Animals with Jobs

Circus Animals

Judith Janda Presnall

KIDHAVEN PRESS™

THOMSON
GALE

San Diego • Detroit • New York • San Francisco • Cleveland
New Haven, Conn. • Waterville Maine • London • Munich

Dedication
This book is dedicated to all circus workers who are involved with the training of and caring for animals. May circus animals have a long future in the education and entertainment of young and old alike.

Acknowledgment
The author thanks Wally Ross, a former Circus Vargas trainer of elephants, ponies, and liberty horses, for his comments and answers.

LIBRARY OF CONGRESS CATALOGING-IN-PUBLICATION DATA

Presnall, Judith Janda.
  Circus animals / by Judith Janda Presnall.
    p. cm.—(Animals with jobs)
Summary: Discusses the use of performing animals in the circus, their training and care both in and out of the ring, and different organizations' monitoring of their treatment.
Includes bibliographical references (p.   ) and index.
  ISBN 0-7377-1360-7 (hardback: alk. paper)
1.Circus animals—Juvenile literature. [1. Circus animals. 2. Working animals. 3. Animals—Training. 4. Animals—Treatment.] I. Title. II. Series.
  GV1829 .P65 2003
  791.3'2—dc21

2002000662

Printed in the United States of America

Contents

Chapter One

Performing Circus Animals

Traveling-show circus animals have jobs that keep them active. Their days are filled with practicing and performing.

Circus Menageries

Circuses have been around for a long time. In the 1930s, circus owners traveled to India and Africa in search of **exotic** animals for their **menageries**. They brought back giraffes, hippopotamuses, lions, snakes, gorillas, Bengal tigers, jaguars, kangaroos, and chimpanzees. For many circus-goers, it was the first time they had ever seen such animals. Today, wild animals are not used in circuses. Most circus animals nowadays are captive-bred.

Today, people still flock to the circus to see beasts such as elephants, tigers, lions, leopards, and horses perform stunts in the center ring.

Big cat trainer Sara Houcke, of the Ringling Brothers and Barnum & Bailey Circus, commands five tigers to sit upright in the center ring.

Why Elephants Make Good Performers

Elephants have been a part of American circuses since the 1880s. Asian elephants are preferred over African elephants because the bigger-eared African elephants are strong willed and less dependable. Usually only female elephants are trained to perform. They generally have pleasant temperaments and enjoy each other's company. Male elephants, because of their aggressive temperament, are not often used in circuses.

Elephants are the largest of all circus animals. One elephant, named Jumbo, weighed almost seven tons. Despite their size, for the most part elephants are **docile**, agile, and affectionate creatures. These highly intelligent animals are capable of learning more than fifty commands.

Trainers use the elephant's natural wild behaviors to train and develop acts. For example, for food in the wild, elephants stand on their hind legs to strip trees of branches with their trunks. They push objects and pick up logs with their trunks. In India, **mahouts** ride elephants during logging work.

Certain animals in the wild behave in a way that allows for natural training. For instance, if an elephant fidgets and squirms a lot, it can be taught to dance. The trainer first throws an old blanket or rug on the elephant's back. The elephant is then rewarded—with food or praise—for shaking it off. Eventually the elephant shimmies and wiggles on command, which makes it look like it is dancing.

Another natural behavior of elephants, standing on their hind legs to strip trees for food, is used in the circus ring. This favorite elephant stunt, called the long mount, is a long line of the huge creatures, each one standing with its hefty forelegs on the back of the elephant in front of it. In the Ringling Brothers and Barnum & Bailey Circus, seventeen elephants form a spectacular line. Other animals, such as big cats, perform in large groups, too.

Big Cats

Lions, tigers, and leopards are known as big cats. Trainer Graham Thomas Chipperfield has an act using eleven female lions and one male lion. His lions are bred and raised on his family farm in Oxfordshire, England. Chipperfield chooses his lions from the group when they

With riders on their shoulders, circus elephants perch on the back of the elephant in front of them in what is known as the long mount.

are one year old and trains them for two years before he uses them in a circus act. Chipperfield selects lion cubs that are noisy and have an aggressive personality. He likes the teeth-bearing lions to display these traits to make his presentation energetic.

Slinky Tigers

Another big circus cat is the tiger. It grows to more than five hundred pounds (about one hundred pounds heavier than the lion). Circuses usually use Siberian or Bengal tigers. Siberians are bigger, more difficult to train, and do not like to be touched. Bengal tigers, however, will tolerate touching. When tigers are between one and four years old, they are easy to build a relationship with and thus easier to train.

One of the tiger's natural abilities, which is used in the circus ring, is standing on its hind legs. Tiger trainer David Tetzlaff explains:

> Standing on hind legs is a natural thing for tigers. It's one way they play as cubs and also fight as adults. In the wild, both animals rear up like ponies, which puts them on equal terms, then one tries to knock the other to the ground. It's a natural aggressive behavior that we're turning into a non-aggressive demonstration for the show.[1]

For example, a tiger may be taught to walk or stand on its hind legs and stretch at full length to retrieve a piece of meat held at the end of a stick. Or it may be trained to dance with its trainer. Varieties of this trick include walking forward and backward, hopping forward, or rotating in a circle.

Spotted Leopards

Other big cats, such as the spotted leopard, black panther, and mountain lion can be taught to do the same tricks as tigers and lions. David Tetzlaff, a world-renowned animal trainer based at Jungle Larry's Caribbean Gardens in Naples, Florida, has trained about twenty leopards in ten years. Tetzlaff explains his feelings about leopards:

> Leopards are so intelligent and clever. It's the beauty of it and the undoing of it. The smarter an

A spotted leopard rests on the shoulders of trainer Gunther Gebel-Williams.

animal is the more ways it thinks of to outsmart you and try to be two or three steps ahead of you, which I like. . . . It makes them harder to train than lions or tigers.[2]

Galloping Horses

Other attractive, graceful animals that commonly appear in American circuses are horses. Some features that trainers look for in horses include intelligence, beauty, and strong legs. Horses working in circuses are at least two years old.

Acrobats perform stunts on the backs of galloping horses called rosinbacks.

Most circus horses in the United States perform two different jobs and are called either rosinbacks or liberty horses. Rosinbacks are named for the rosin dust that is sprinkled on their backs to give performers surer footing. They carry bareback riders and acrobats. They are usually Percheron or Belgian horses because these animals have sturdy, broad backs. Acrobats also use stallions because of their high speed and strength.

For liberty acts, smaller horses such as Arabians are used. The independent liberty horses perform riderless

A liberty horse dances in the spotlight to the commands of its trainer.

and without restraint. They perform in groups of six to twelve, trotting in circles, doing reverse turns, and standing on their hind legs. The plumed horses, with brushed manes and tails flying, are guided through formations and tricks by a trainer using two whips. The inborn actions of trotting, galloping, and rearing up on their hind legs are natural behaviors for untamed horses. Circus animal trainers use the animals' natural behaviors when teaching stunts.

Chapter Two

Training Circus Animals

Circus animal trainers learn their skills from family members in the business or by observing and working with other trainers. A successful trainer must be courageous, with a flair for showmanship, as well as be physically fit, cool-headed, and exceptionally patient. But above all, the trainer must love animals.

Animal Variations

Just like humans, each animal is different. Some are smarter than others, some are more cooperative, and some are lazy. Some have fears. For example, some tigers are afraid of fire. No amount of training can make them jump through a hoop of flames.

Training animals requires mutual respect between teacher and animal. Mark Oliver Gebel, the son of world-renowned animal trainer Gunther Gebel-Williams, has been with Ringling since he came to the circus

Standing among large elephants, a trainer works under dangerous conditions.

grounds after being released from the hospital after he was three days old. Gebel says, "You can't force an animal to do anything. That's the bottom line. Forcing an animal to do anything only builds resentment and can lead to dangerous situations."[3]

For trainers, there is always an element of danger when working with their animals. They put their lives on the line daily.

Gunther Gebel-Williams

Gunther Gebel-Williams, of Ringling, pioneered a way of working with circus animals that is used by many trainers today. Gebel-Williams, who died in 2001, had a special fascination and harmony with animals. He believed that unending patience was the secret in training any animal. His rules were: Never strike an animal, constantly repeat instructions, use rewards for successes, and give only a mild scolding for failure.

A trainer hugs and kisses her horses. Trainers must have patience, respect, and love for their animals.

Known as "Lord of the Rings," Gebel-Williams trained a large variety of animals: fifty to sixty tigers; thirty-five leopards, black panthers, mountain lions; ten lions; fifty elephants; hundreds of horses; llamas; camels; and zebras. Practice and performance is important in learning how to train animals. Most trainers spend fifteen hours a day at their craft, including caring for their animals.

With the help of many standby assistants, Gebel-Williams could direct a herd of thirty-two elephants by voice. Sometimes the elephants were paraded up a street from the train yard to the arena. Other times the elephants would be in three rings and he would yell commands at them from forty feet away. Gebel-Williams says

> To train my animals, I used words, always words. I'd say, "Come here," to any one of the elephants, and it would walk right over to me. They knew the command "Pick it up," spoken during an animal walk or exercise session, meant they had to quicken their pace. And they all understood the word "Good."[4]

His technique is remarkable for two reasons: First, Ringling is the only circus in the United States with such a large herd of elephants. Second, most other trainers use a hook to guide animals in a specific direction. But trainers also use a hook for protection for themselves, and audiences, and to protect elephants from each other, in case they get out of control.

Gebel-Williams believed he was successful because he cared about his animals the way he cared about his friends. He noted in an interview:

Gunther Gebel-Williams hugs a large spotted leopard, one of the many animals he trained during his long career.

I am the boss, but they know I am also their friend. I feel very close to my animals. If I miss a morning with them, I feel bad. Once you become totally involved with the animals, they become a part of you. . . . They are like my family.[5]

Tiger Stunts

Tigers can be trained to sit up, roll over individually and as a group, play leapfrog, walk in an orderly line, leap through fire hoops, hold fire sticks in their mouths, and walk forward and backward on their hind legs.

Because a tiger's razorlike claws can easily tear human skin, they are dangerous to work with. Trainers take many risks when they teach wild, or untamed, animals. (Whether born in the wild or in captivity, most circus beasts retain their instincts.)

The Stages of Training a Tiger

Tiger training takes place under relatively quiet conditions, but the animals must eventually adapt to the unique circus atmosphere. They must learn to ignore loud music, bright lights, and the shouting, applauding spectators.

When cubs are about eleven months old, trainers condition them by allowing them to view the performance from their private cages inside the arena. Their cages are rolled into the arena, where they can absorb the show's environment. This exposes the trainees to the noise and lights, but from the security of their cages. The next step is to move the tigers from their individual cages to the performance cage in the arena. They then spend several

Sara Houcke comforts a young white tiger in a side ring to help the animal adjust to the circus atmosphere.

months merely sitting on a **pedestal** (a high stool in the big cage) watching the experienced tigers perform.

At fifteen months of age, the tiger is ready for actual training. The trainer rolls the tiger's cage up to the animal entrance of the performance cage. The tiger's **chute** door is opened and the animal is allowed into the performance ring.

With the trainer holding two sticks—a pointed metal rod for meat, and the other a stout wooden stick for cues—the trainer and the tiger begin their first lesson together. Training sessions last only forty-five minutes so that both trainer and tiger do not get overly tired.

The trainer keeps the tiger's chute door open so if the animal becomes frightened, it knows there is a way to escape. The tiger may become spooked by a number of things, including noises and other animals. An escape route keeps the tiger from feeling trapped.

The trainer talks constantly to the animal so it becomes accustomed to the tone of his or her voice. The tiger is also frequently rewarded with bits of fresh meat for doing what the trainer commands.

Seat Breaking

The first exercise for the tiger is seat breaking, or training a tiger to sit on a pedestal. A steel pedestal ranges from eighteen to sixty inches high with the seat about twenty inches square. The trainer, using meat rewards and verbal praises, teaches the tiger to jump to the pedestal from the floor, sit on its **haunches**, and stay there. It takes about three days for the tiger to learn this lesson. But seat breaking is not complete until the trainer is certain that the animal, once seated, will not move under any circumstances unless it is commanded or cued to leave.

Seat breaking is important so that the tiger does not sneak up on the trainer or try to attack other tigers when a stressful situation occurs. During a circus performance in Italy, the circus's power plant abruptly shut down in the middle of a tiger act, plunging the stage into total darkness.

The trainer, in the center of a cage full of tigers, could see nothing. He kept yelling and repeating "Seat!" and each tiger's name. When the lights flashed back on, the

Two trainers work with a tiger cub to teach it vital lessons necessary to become a circus cat.

trainer was relieved to find all eight of his tigers faithfully sitting on their assigned seats.

Training Elephants

Elephants begin their training at about three years of age and can work until about fifty-five years old. Elephants may be trained singly or in groups of two or three. They are given verbal commands and guided with a hook to get them to lift a leg or turn in a particular direction.

With repetition, the elephants learn to associate each command with a different action. The stunts that elephants can be taught include standing on their heads, sitting on stools or barrels, dancing, and standing on their hind legs.

A young girl helps train baby elephants to sit upright on stools. Elephant training begins at about age three.

Gebel-Williams explains the dangers of working with elephants:

> People love elephants, but if something happens suddenly—a train goes by; a truck backfires; a bat, pigeon, or mouse gets in their tent—they can either explode or continue to be gentle and do nothing. If something goes wrong in their minds, even if they have worked with you for twenty years, elephants can hurt or kill you.[6]

Years of meticulous training are required behind the scenes before a circus act can finally be performed.

Chapter Three

Circus Animals on the Job

When the lights come on, animals and their trainers are ready to perform and impress the crowd with their talents. Their performances reflect a bond between human and beast.

Stunts in the Steel Cage

For all their beauty, power, and grace, big cats still have instincts and are dangerous and deadly. When performers enter the steel cage, they depend on their courage, skill, and mutual trust.

Big cats are not declawed or defanged for the circus. They are not drugged. Because they are motivated by food, animals are fed during and after the performance.

Charly Baumann was a cage boy (someone who works, grooms, and cleans up after the animals) for two years in Europe before starting his circus career with horses and elephants. When he came to the United States, Baumann pioneered many big cat acts while working for Ringling Brothers from 1964 to 1983. Baumann performed such stunts as growling tigers walking on a double tightrope; paw-waving tigers balancing on their haunches on high pedestals above mirrored revolving globes; two limber tigers jumping simultaneously through two fire-wrapped hoops; and six orange-and-black-striped tigers performing a double rollover.

Baumann also presented a mixed act of lions and tigers. The two big cat species do not get along in the wild. When a tiger actually attacked Baumann in the cage during a performance, a lion attacked the tiger and made it appear that he was saving Baumann's life. However, the lion really just took the opportunity to attack his natural enemy. Not all went well during Baumann's circus career.

A Stunt Backfires

One stunt that went wrong used a lion as part of an advertising campaign. Circus Bügler, a circus in Germany, once asked Baumann, its lion tamer, to put his head in a lion's mouth as photographers snapped pictures. Baumann remembers the first time he performed this publicity stunt:

> That afternoon when Nero [Baumann's male lion] opened his mouth during the act, he must have been terribly surprised. I dropped to my knees, grabbed his jaws with both hands and held them open as I shoved my head into his mouth. The trick, as I came to realize, was not really dan-

gerous if you got your head into the animal's mouth quickly enough. While it was between the jaws he couldn't exert much pressure.[7]

A performer at the Milan circus imitates Charly Baumann's act, sticking his face in a lion's mouth.

However, Nero did not put up with this act for long and eventually rebelled. One day Nero put his paw on top of Baumann's skull and pushed it further inside his mouth, closing his jaws tighter and tighter. Nero's fangs had bloodied Baumann's face by the time the trainer was finally able to pry the lion's jaws apart and free his head.

A Tiger Shows His Viciousness

Big cats could attack at any time, even during a show, as trainer Wade Burck experienced. Unlike many performers, Burck did not come from a circus family. After graduation from high school in North Dakota, the young man served a five-year training apprenticeship in the circus before performing with tigers. He even slept in a sleeping bag on top of the tiger cages to establish a close relationship with them.

In 1980, twenty-five-year-old Wade Burck was mauled by Frosty, one of his white tigers. During a show in Boston, Massachusetts, Burck tried to break up a fight between Frosty and another tiger. A petrified audience watched in horror as Frosty let go of the other tiger and lunged at Burck. Frosty wrapped his huge jaws around his trainer's face. The tiger dragged Burck around the cage over the backs of four other tigers. Next, Frosty bit through Burck's right shoulder, punctured an artery, and broke his collarbone. Frosty continued to shake his trainer like a rag doll.

Burck said later that during the struggle he prayed to die. "Lord, if I got to die, strike me dead now, 'cause it hurts so bad and I don't want to suffer no more."[8]

Before a performance, Sara Houcke hugs and kisses a huge white tiger as it enters the center ring.

But someone finally pushed a stick into Frosty's mouth while others pulled the tiger off Burck. The bleeding Burck was rushed to the hospital, where his wounds were bandaged and his jaw wired. It is rumored in the circus world that Frosty stayed with Burck's act after this attack. Committed to his animals, Burck continued with tiger training and performing for several years after this episode.

Trainers Use Different Techniques

Sara Houcke is a seventh-generation performer from Europe. When Houcke began training tigers, the felines accepted her right away. Houcke recalls:

I had to clean cages at first just to get contact, to know each individual's character. . . . My act is more about relationship. This isn't about me sticking my head in their mouths and proving I'm the strong one. It's about trust. . . . I've never been nervous. The tigers respect the word "no."[9]

Houcke made her tiger act debut with the Ringling Brothers circus at age twenty-three. Houcke hugs and kisses each of her seven Bengal tigers as they enter the spotlighted steel mesh cage in the center ring. Though Houcke is aware of the danger, she puts it out of her mind during her eight-minute act.

Houcke uses kindness and gentleness to coax her five-hundred-pound tigers to sit on their haunches and beg, lie down, and roll over. She rewards them with a pat on the head and a hunk of raw meat fed to them from her hand, not on a stick as other trainers do.

Beastly Elephants Show Off

Unlike the furry, naturally beautiful big cats, the huge gray elephants are groomed to look their best. Their wrinkled skin is scrubbed, tough toenails clipped, crusty eyelids coated with petroleum jelly, and their heads and backs are decoratively costumed. One crowd-pleasing stunt is the pyramid: One elephant stands on the ground or on a stool with an elephant on each side. The elephants on each side place their forelegs on the back of the center elephant. A human stands on the back of the lowest elephant. Sometimes the elephants stand on stools to elevate themselves in the triangle.

Elephants with performers on their backs stand on their hind legs on top of small tools.

Ringling Brothers elephant trainer Graham Thomas Chipperfield perfected a teeterboard takeoff trick using two elephants. The stunt took a year and a half of training and practice. First, an elephant was taught to strike a teeterboard with just the right amount of pressure. In the beginning, Chipperfield used a one-hundred-fifty-pound bundle of hay (his weight) on the teeterboard.

Five different teeterboards were built before one was just right. Then Chipperfield, wearing a mechanic safety belt, practiced forward jumps and backward somersaults. Chipperfield used a second elephant who would stand still for his landing. In the final presentation, Chipperfield stood on one side of the teeterboard while one elephant stomped the other end, flipping the trainer somersaulting into the air and onto the back of the standing elephant.

An Elephant on a Rampage

Sometimes an elephant can go on a rampage for no apparent reason. In 1992, Kelly, a twenty-seven-year-old female Asian elephant, was part of the preshow for the Great American Circus. She ferried riders on her back. During one ill-fated event in Palm Bay, Florida, six passengers were riding in the **howdah**, or platform, atop Kelly's back when the eight-thousand-pound animal suddenly bashed into a cage wall.

The usually docile Kelly ignored her trainer's commands. Instead, she wildly swung her trunk, hurling the surprised trainer across the ring. The passengers—a woman and five children—clung to the howdah and screamed in terror.

Some of the spectators scrambled for the exits. Kelly ripped cables and overhead wires before she left the tent. She then turned her rage on a nearby car, trying to tip it over. Fortunately, a policeman and a circus worker momentarily distracted Kelly, allowing the people on her back to escape.

Kelly then continued her rampage by attacking a van. She tore the skin of her trunk while smashing the van's windshield and door. When Kelly headed back into the tent where more than two thousand spectators remained, the police knew they would have to shoot the out-of-control elephant. Officers shot about twenty-

Children run in mock terror and clear a path for an unrestrained elephant. The large animals are dangerous when spooked.

five times before the elephant finally toppled on her side.

Although this was a sad ending for Kelly, audiences thrill in the mystical rapport between trainers and animals and the delicate balance of beauty and danger. The bonds of caretaker go beyond performing under the big top. Trainers make sure that their animals are safe after their years of service.

Chapter Four

Retirement of Circus Animals

Eventually, all animals become too old to perform and travel with a circus. Trainers then try to find pleasant, safe homes where their animals can live out their lives comfortably. When circus animals are ready for retirement, they are placed in a variety of **sanctuaries** and retreats throughout the United States. Some circuses donate their retired animals to zoos.

Temporary Retirement

When Gebel-Williams stopped performing with his tigers, he put them into temporary retirement at the Venice, Florida, winter quarters. However, he did not ignore them. He exercised the tigers regularly and gave them the same care as usual:

> I tried to keep my animals working as long as they were healthy and strong. Once they started getting old, I took them out of the acts so that they did

not have to work hard, but some of them balked at losing their status as performers. This happened with a tiger named India, who was with me more than twenty years. From the first day of her retirement, India cried every time I passed her by and brought other tigers into the ring.[10]

One day Gebel-Williams decided to let India back into the act. Another tiger noticed that India was a little shaky and he jumped down from his pedestal and bit India very hard on the neck. India almost died. It is the nature of

Two circus tigers play with a keeper in a zoo where they were placed to retire comfortably.

tigers to attack weaker animals that cannot defend themselves. Animals that are old and weak need to be cared for in special places.

The Elephant Sanctuary

Circus elephants often work until they are in their late fifties. Ringling Brothers donates their retired elephants to zoos. Circus Vargas retired their African elephant, Ruby, to the Los Angeles Zoo. With good care, elephants may live for sixty to seventy years (compared to thirty-five years in the wild). One retirement home designed specifically for old, sick, or needy female elephants that have been retired from circuses, zoos, and other show business acts is The Elephant Sanctuary.

The sanctuary, located in Hohenwald, Tennessee, opened in 1995. It is the nation's only natural refuge developed to meet the needs of **endangered** Asian elephants. The retirement home is situated on 800 acres and has room for a herd of twelve. At this time, the elephants have unlimited access on 222 acres of natural habitat.

The animals wander at will, wallow in mud, graze for bamboo and hickory, and just live like elephants—no longer required to perform or entertain the public. Five workers provide round-the-clock care. The habitat includes a stream, three spring-fed ponds, and 150 varieties of trees and vegetation for elephant munching. A specialized barn comes complete with automatic watering devices, heated floors, and an automated manure-removal system.

Two retired elephants wear custom-made earmuffs to protect them from the cold at The Elephant Sanctuary in Tennessee.

Riddle's Elephant Breeding Farm and Sanctuary

In 1990, Scott and Heidi Riddle established a sanctuary located on 330 acres in the Ozark Mountain foothills in Greenbrier, Arkansas. This internationally recognized sanctuary accepts any elephant regardless of species, gender, or disposition. The animals are retirees from circuses, various zoological institutions, or private ownership.

At this sanctuary, people can make weekend reservations to have an up-close encounter with elephants. The

Retired elephants wait for their weekly bath during Riddle's Elephant Breeding Farm and Sanctuary's up-close weekend encounter.

weekend activities begin on a Friday, with visitors meeting the staff and the elephants. On Saturday and Sunday, participants feed and water all of the elephants, learn to trim toenails, bathe an elephant, and help with research observations.

Wildlife on Easy Street

Lions and tigers also have their own retirement homes. After working until about age fifteen, some may retire to

Wildlife on Easy Street, located in Tampa, Florida. The forty-acre sanctuary houses more than 170 exotic cats. Of this number, six are retired from Ringling Brothers, which pays for their continued care.

The facility offers a program called Expedition Easy Street, in which people can interact with the large felines. Guests, eighteen years or older, stay in cabins on the grounds and may be lulled to sleep by the roaring and calling of lions and tigers. Participants work as volunteers with staff members. They can hand-feed fruit to certain cats and interact with smaller felines inside their enclosures.

A lioness playfully paws another lioness in the Wildlife on Easy Street retirement facility for large cats in Tampa, Florida.

Mill Creek Farm

Mill Creek Farm boards more than one hundred horses from a variety of sources. Mary and Peter Gregory created this equine sanctuary in 1984 in Alachua, Florida. The haven provides a retirement setting with hundreds of acres of serene, tree-filled, rolling pastures.

Horses perform in circuses for sixteen to twenty years before they retire. At least four of the horses at Mill

Retired horses graze in one of the twenty-one pastures provided by Mill Creek Farm owners Mary and Peter Gregory.

Creek Farm are retirees from the Clyde Beatty/Cole Brothers Circus. In addition, Ringling Brothers may soon be retiring one of their horses to Mill Creek Farm.

During their lives as performers, circus animals share their beauty, form, and skills. Even in retirement, they make an impact by heightening people's interest in endangered species and the need to protect them.

Notes

Chapter One: Performing Circus Animals

1. Quoted in Sharon Rendell, *Living with Big Cats.* Naples, FL: International Zoological Society, 1995, p. 29.
2. Quoted in Rendell, *Living with Big Cats,* p. 41.

Chapter Two: Training Circus Animals

3. Quoted in Renee Graham, "Growing Up in the Greatest Show on Earth," *Boston Globe,* October 12, 1994, p. 69.
4. Gunther Gebel-Williams, *Untamed.* New York: William Morrow, 1991, p. 22.
5. Quoted in John Culhane, "World's Greatest Showman," *Reader's Digest,* November 1989, p. 93.
6. Gebel-Williams, *Untamed,* p. 334.

Chapter Three: Circus Animals on the Job

7. Charly Baumann, *Tiger Tiger.* Chicago: Playboy Press, 1975, pp. 67–68.
8. Quoted in Dan Geringer, "Now He's the Cat's Meow," *Sports Illustrated,* July 21, 1986, p. 35.
9. Quoted in Paula Chin and Bob Meadows, "Burning Bright," *People,* April 17, 2000, pp. 137–38.

Chapter Four: Retirement of Circus Animals

10. Gebel-Williams, *Untamed,* p. 310.

Glossary

chute: An enclosed passageway leading from the big cats' cages to the center ring.

docile: Easily managed, teachable.

endangered: In danger of becoming extinct.

exotic: From another part of the world.

haunches: The hips, buttocks, and upper thighs of an animal.

howdah: A platform or seat on an elephant's back used for carrying people.

mahout: A person who trains and rides working elephants, especially in southern India where elephants are used in the logging industry.

menagerie: A collection of wild animals on display to the public.

pedestal: A strong stool for lions or tigers to sit upon in the center ring.

sanctuary: Place of protection for animals.

Organizations
to Contact

The Elephant Sanctuary
PO Box 393
Hohenwald, TN 38462
(931) 796-6500
www.elephants.com
Some of the information on the website includes photos
of the sanctuary, a description of the sanctuary's goals,
plus biographies and photos of the elephants.

Mill Creek Farm
PO Box 2100
Alachua, FL 32616-2100
(386) 462-1001
www.millcreekfarm.org
This website reports that Mill Creek Farm boards more
than one hundred retired horses. The horses receive individual attention, food, grooming, and veterinary care
at this equine sanctuary.

Ringling Brothers and Barnum & Bailey Circus
www.ringling.com
This website details many aspects of animals including
training and performance of elephants, big cats, and

horses, as well as transportation, backstage, and the Center for Elephant Conservation.

Wildlife on Easy Street
12802 Easy Street
Tampa, FL 33625
(813) 920-4130
www.wildlifeeasyst.com
The website describes the sanctuary, which cares for more than 170 exotic cats, including lions, tigers, and bear cats. The public can tour, interact, and even spend the night in the middle of the haven.

For Further Exploration

Bruce Feiler, "Ringling Rehearses," *Life,* April 1999. Portrays in photographs how "The Greatest Show on Earth" gets its act together.

Martin Hintz, *Tons of Fun: Training Elephants.* New York: Julian Messner, 1982. Traces the history of elephants in American zoos and circuses and describes the art of handling and training them.

Judith Janda Presnall, *Circuses.* New York: Franklin Watts, 1996. Describes how circuses got their start and what is happening under the big top today.

Lynn Saville, *Horses in the Circus Ring.* New York: E.P. Dutton, 1989. Reports how circus horses are trained to perform a variety of feats, including precision teamwork, carrying a pyramid of humans, and stunt riding.

Big Cats of the Big Top. Ringling Brothers and Barnum & Bailey, Family Home Entertainment, 1987. This sixty-minute video interviews three tiger trainers: Gunther Gebel-Williams, Charly Baumann, and Wade Burck. It shows each of the performers in the ring with their tigers.

Index

Picture Credits

About the Author

Judith Janda Presnall is an award-winning nonfiction writer. Besides the Animals with Jobs series, her books include *Rachel Carson, Artificial Organs, The Giant Panda, Oprah Winfrey, Mount Rushmore, Life on Alcatraz, Animals That Glow, Animal Skeletons,* and *Circuses.* Presnall graduated from the University of Wisconsin in Whitewater. She is a recipient of the Jack London Award for meritorious service in the California Writers Club. She is also a member of the Society of Children's Book Writers and Illustrators. Judith lives in the Los Angeles area with her husband, Lance, and three cats.